Epic Bear Adult Coloring Book

I0410405

BY SUSAN POTTERFIELDS

ISBN: 10: 154033967X
ISBN- 13: 978-1540339676

LETTERS

Susan Potterfields is a digital artist. You can find more of her work on Amazon and digitalcoloringbooks.com.

www.ingramcontent.com/pod-product-compliance
Lightning Source LLC
Chambersburg PA
CBHW081806280526
45789CB00008B/3019
* 9 7 8 1 5 4 0 3 3 9 6 7 6 *